D1089077

PERSONAL PORTRAITS

Edited by Patric Dickinson and Sheila Shannon

SIR TOBIE MATHEW by DAVID MATHEW

DAVID MATHEW

SIR TOBIE MATHEW

with eight plates in photogravure
eight illustrations in line

MAX PARRISH LONDON

1950

MAX PARRISH & CO LTD
Adprint House Rathbone Place London W 1
in association with
CHANTICLEER PRESS INC
41 East 50th Street New York 22 N Y
ADPRINT LIMITED LONDON

The text of this book is set in Monotype Garamond 11 on 12 pt
Printed in Great Britain by Clarke & Sherwell Ltd Northampton

CONTENTS

ILLUSTRATIONS IN LINE

PLATES IN PHOTOGRAVURE

ACKNOWLEDGMENTS

Grateful acknowledgment is due to the following for permission to reproduce illustrations in this book:

Facing pages 16, 17, 33
The Trustees of the National Portrait Gallery

Facing page 32
The Corsini Gallery, Florence, and Messrs. Alinari

Facing page 48 (top)
The Director of the Victoria & Albert Museum

Facing pages 49, 65
The Trustees of the British Museum

Facing page 64
Lt.-Col. H. G. Sotheby

The portraits of the Duke of Buckingham and of John Donne, facing page 48, are reproduced by gracious permission of H. M. The King

THE GRAND TOUR

He was the close disciple and confidant of Francis Bacon. He made the first English translation of the *Confessions of St. Augustine*. He was long a figure at the English Court and sensitive to its transitions. His account of his submission to the Church of Rome stands almost at the head of the long series of recitals of such conversions. He was one of the great European travellers of his day, always along the highways of privileged travel. He was in some respects the very type of the cosmopolitan Englishman of his place and century. His character has always puzzled and eluded me, and this is an attempt to disentangle the complex strands.

Sir Tobie Mathew was born at Salisbury a little after three of the clock in the afternoon of 3 October 1577 to Frances, wife of Dr. Tobie Mathew, at that time Dean of Christ Church, Archdeacon of Bath and Prebendary of Teynton Regis in Salisbury Cathedral. By subsequent promotions Tobie Mathew the elder attained the deanery and bishopric of Durham and finally the archbishopric of York. Frances Mathew was the widow of Matthew Parker, second son of the Archbishop of Canterbury of the same names, and the third daughter of William Barlow, Bishop of Chichester. Both parents survived to extreme old age, dying in 1628 and 1629; they thus dominated Tobie's life, controlling the purse strings and in the last resort protecting him. It is perhaps permissible to trace in Tobie Mathew that wistful immaturity which at times attaches to a man who has no fixed income but whose family and friends are always good to him. His youth was thus prolonged unnaturally, for he was already just on forty-six when the favourite, Buckingham, described him as "little prittie Tobie Mathew". Such were his circumstances.

Tobie Mathew was, it would seem, a natural traveller, as his generation understood that polite activity. He was among the first to take those roads along which the coaches and chariots of English *milords* were soon to follow. Such journeys were not precisely confined to movements between court and court, but needless halts were seldom made except at provincial capitals. Inevitably there was an urban character about such travel. Even at this time we can trace the emphasis upon that norm of the practice of society on which Lord Chesterfield would later lay such stress. Something of its nature and of its stiff *formulae* can be suggested by describing it as the extended experience of a series of *milieux* which were linked up and analogous.

At this time there was hardly any reference to scenery; it was difficult to render with the necessary formalism. Archaeological enquiry was still rare. The avowed purpose was normally to study the

The only known portrait of Tobie Mathew forms the frontis-piece of the 'Collection of Letters' published together with his 'Character of the Countess' in 1660, five years after his death.

cities and institutions of foreign States and to gain proficiency in their languages by converse with one's social equals. The actual journeys were interesting in so far as they were illumined by exchanges with men of quality encountered on the way. In Tobie Mathew's case there was however a difference, for he had a nostalgia for the Continent and the great monarchies. In this connection it is interesting to try to place him.

It may be suggested that throughout the period of almost two hundred years between the death of Queen Elizabeth in 1603 and the outbreak of the French Revolution travel to the countries of Western Europe was continuous. The road to Paris might be closed in time of war, but the way that led through Brussels into Germany was always open. There was traffic between Ostend and the "Spaw" throughout the seventeenth and eighteenth centuries. This town in the bishopric of Liége was to give its name to every other spa that would develop. The search for health came first, but the opportunities for gambling soon detained the interest of men of quality. The same facilities became available wherever persons of standing gathered to take the waters. In 1635 it was reported that Lord Dunluce lost almost £2,000 at ninepins to Sir John Suckling at the Wells at Tunbridge. Still in these years when the Archduke Albert and the Archduchess Isabella ruled in Brussels the element of gambling formed a private recreation. The professional gambler belongs rather to the Restoration period, and the bird of prey did not arrive upon the scene until the time of the Chevalier de Balibari in *Barry Lyndon.* In

Tobie Mathew's day the search for health, a form of unofficial diplomatic contact, the purchase of luxuries and works of art were principal motives for these foreign journeys. Each year the heavy coaches carrying their load of English travellers plunged through the dusty tracks across those plains which had been known as Flanders and Brabant and were then called the lands of the Archdukes' Obedience, and later the Spanish and then the Austrian Netherlands.

It was upon the basis of such easy journeying that the more extended travel was developed. The outlines of the well-known routes to Italy were gradually set out and a definite fashion was established. Tobie stood at the very beginning of this tradition. He was only nine years younger than Sir Henry Wotton. He was among those who took their part in laying down the careful rubric of the Grand Tour.

It is clear that his interests were channelled and it seems that he had no great grasp outside the sphere of politics, while within this field his views in time became quite stereotyped. What was remarkable was his sensitive literary adaptability. He had a good ear and spoke Italian perfectly. His talent matured in a foreign mould that lay prepared for it. He was never in the ordinary sense an Englishman Italianate. He had a sweet singing voice and liked love songs and madrigals. By nature he was suited to the years of peace.

It has often seemed to me strange that Tobie does not appear to have been associated with Essex House. It is true that when he was eighteen years old he acted the esquire's part in Essex's "device" on the Queen's day. Still there is no sign that any intimacy developed. There is likewise little evidence of a special link with the more elegant among his contemporaries at Christ Church. Traditionally Tobie is said to have been a "noted orator and disputant" in his Oxford years. For certain reasons Essex would possibly not have been prepared to offer to bring him into his friendship. The Bishop of Durham had always been acceptable to the Cecils, who were Essex's enemies. Perhaps there was already Francis Bacon.

In addition it is worth remembering that Essex and his friends, although susceptible to foreign and especially to Italian influences, were in no sense travellers. In no period has the English ruling class had less personal experience of the Continent than in the second half of Elizabeth's reign. The war with Spain, the presence of the Guise faction in France and the sharp conflict with the Papacy were factors which would discourage travel. Besides, the Elizabethan mood was self-sufficient and glorious. It was natural that foreigners should come to the Queen's court to seek for patrons.

Viewed from this angle the life of the great Elizabethan lords, Leicester and Essex as examples, seems almost static, for they were burdened by their own great households, their friends and their attendant gentlemen. In the nature of things Essex and his entourage were only attracted overseas by profitable war. It was the prospect of the sack of Cadiz or the advantages expected from the Island Voyage which would empty Essex House of the

Earl's friends and dependants. Under such stimulus they would crowd into the ships.

There are detailed descriptions of that voyage to Cadiz. The scene has an unrestrained Elizabethan splendour as the *Due Repulse* sails south on the expedition which would bring so great a profit. The young men crowd about their patron, while the more experienced soldiers make their plans. In the great cabin Essex keeps his state; his equals are around him and the secretaries behind them. The magnificent man can now reward even his meanest follower. The next panel has the same quality a trifle heightened. Essex sits in his armed chair as the ship moves northward. The friends around him speak in suitable terms about his glory. His secretary, known as the "Grecian" Cuffe, turns happy phrases touched with erudition. Stacked in the fore cabin stand rare books, for the General has himself accepted the Bishop of Algarve's library which certain of the mariners have brought on board. The gentlemen, bareheaded from respect, stand silently working out their profits; they lack a merchant's training to assess the silks and pearls.

Down in the hold the rats nibble at the wooden chests now stored with treasure. It is hot below and the men grow quarrelsome as each keeps guard upon his master's boxes. In the great cabin manners are urbane, and the west wind blowing up from the Azores lightens the oppressive summer weather. Behind each compliment there lies a challenging vinous optimism.

The picture is drawn in close detail to show that here there was no place for Tobie Mathew. There was no place either for Francis Bacon, so sceptical in regard to his contemporaries. For Tobie wholly escaped the grand Elizabethan emphasis perhaps because he lived so very near to it. He seems to have been a rather precise young man; his wit was measured. He was a great disappointment to his father. It is time to examine the relations between the two men in so far as we can now discern the situation.

The character of Tobie Mathew the elder contains few surprises. He was easy and circumspect, a prelate of business, a man whom the world had treated well. His public life is fairly well documented and there is also a manuscript diary. He began very early on his chosen course, for he was only thirteen years of age when he entered University College; it was at the time when the Elizabethan Settlement was first established. He was twenty when he gained the Queen's attention disputing before her in St. Mary's Church. The Christ Church portrait hardly suggests the fresh and slender figure that first attracted her. "He was much respected", explained Anthony à Wood, collecting fragments of tradition, "for his great learning, eloquence, sweet conversation and the sharpness of his wit." Nothing came really to disturb that quiet-tempered serenity. He seems to have kept through life a sense of the ridiculous and of the unbecoming. "He was", wrote Fuller in his *Church History*, "of a cheerful spirit yet without any trespass on episcopal gravity, there lying a real distinction between facetiousness and nugacity."

Everything had come to him so very swiftly. At

Tobie Mathew the elder, Archbishop of York, at the age of seventy, painted by an unknown artist.

PLATE I

Francis Bacon, Baron Verulam and Viscount St. Albans.

PLATE II

twenty-six he was president of St. John's, admittedly a poor foundation, at thirty he received the deanery of Christ Church, at thirty-three he was Vice-Chancellor. He was always proud to be "ex Cambria oriundus"; it may have been his Welsh descents that gave the turn for oratory. At thirty-seven he was promoted to the deanery of Durham and began his forty years of administration in the North. That was in 1583, when his eldest son Tobie was six years old.

He had written against Campion's *Decem Rationes* and had no patience with the Recusants. It was repugnant to him that men should disallow the Queen's religion. While he studied the workings of what was then termed the "Bishoprick", and later when he himself administered that great Durham Palatinate, it became manifest that the more stiff-necked Papists struck at both spiritual and temporal authority. In consequence he viewed with favour the Church-Papists, who were particularly numerous in the first half of his episcopate. These were gentlemen of Catholic sympathies who understood that attendance at worship as prescribed by law was only seemly in those whose worldly station would entitle them to a place in the commission of the peace. Towards such men the Bishop was genial and emollient. As he grew older it came to him more clearly that it was against decency that the Queen should be defied.

He himself belonged to a Catholic family, but the career which he had chosen detached him from his kinsmen. The foreign world did not appeal to him. In his celebrated defence of the Reformation there is no mention of Luther. He only accepted innovations which came with royal authority. His opinion of the modern Roman Church was low, and this was perhaps the fruit of his many cheerful talks with Alberico Gentili, whom he protected. He had a profound dislike for all the busy priests who smuggled themselves into his diocese from overseas.

His relations with the great Elizabethan statesmen were appreciative rather than intimate. His career was divided into halves, first Oxford and then administration in the northern bishoprics. He had received favours from both wings of the Queen's advisers, from Leicester and from the Cecil grouping. He was not in any exact sense a courtier and his dignified yet remote employments had always secured him respectful treatment. It seems that he set great store by this last point. His marriage had at the time been prudent, but perhaps had he waited he would have allied himself with a different circle. He kept up good relations with the lords president at York and had more sympathy with the problems of the lay administrators in the wild northern country than with the preoccupations of his brethren of the cloth.

He had hardly any experience of what the English scene was like before the Queen's accession. There is no evidence that his schooling at Wells in the years of the restored Mass left any mark on him. In any case there were diverse opinions in that cathedral city in Mary's time. Tobie Mathew the elder always felt that need for uniformity in the politico-religious structure which characterized the thought of his contemporaries. In England the prince would give a native form to the church order. The force of Lord Burghley's wisdom came to him.

Although he was to outlive James I and to receive the northern primacy at his hands, the Archbishop always remained Elizabethan. It seems that he had a horror of all those who might disturb the Queen's tranquillity and her good ordering. Like others among his colleagues on the Anglican episcopal bench, he resembled those Spanish clerics who wasted no thought on the barbarous penalties when the malefactors had passed to the secular arm. He was a scholar along conventional lines but primarily an administrator in a great epoch; he was always fully aware of this greatness. He was hospitable and reasonably generous. In his old age as a little shrunken grey-bearded prelate he kept the dignity of an older fashion. He was ever imperturbable and, when not crossed, sweet-tempered.

This is not a very distinct impression, but it is as close as we are likely to reach to Tobie's father. In regard to Tobie's mother a single sharp description has survived. There are no letters. This scarcity of detail affects the domestic life of almost all the members of the Queen's episcopate. The picture of the bishop is sometimes clear and occasionally also that of the bishop's sons, but never those of the bishop's wife or the bishop's daughters. We therefore cannot reconstruct the lives of the Barlow women, and this applies not only to Frances Mathew but equally to her four sisters, Anne wife of the Bishop of Hereford, Margaret wife of the Bishop of Lichfield, and Elizabeth and Antonia who were wives to successive Bishops of Winchester. Much of our information is recorded in the long inscription to be found on her monument in York Minster:

. . . She was Daughter
Of William Barlow,
Bishop of Chichester;
And, in King Henry the Eighth's time,
Ambassador into Scotland,
Of the antient family
Of the Barlows in Wales.
She had four Sisters
Married to Four Bishops.
One to William Wickham
Bishop of Winchester;
Another to Overton,
Bishop of Coventry and Litchfield;
A third to Westphaling,
Bishop of Hereford;
And a fourth to Day,
That succeeded Wickham, in Winchester.
So that a Bishop was her Father,
An Archbishop her Father-in-Law;
She had Four Bishops, her Brethren,
And an Archbishop her husband . . .

The only personal comment on Mrs. Mathew is from the pen of her eldest son, who did not greatly care for her. "My mother", he wrote in his later years, "was much more fervent [than the Archbishop] towards the Puritanical sole-Scripture way, and was ever upon all occasions wont to be as busy with Scripture as if it had been some glove upon her fingers' ends." She was always suspicious of her child's backsliding.

With his father Tobie had much closer contact. A certain native shrewdness was common to both men, and a capacity for managing in several worlds. Neither was original in political thought, but both refracted as in a mirror ideas of their contemporaries. They were alike in possessing an almost heroic reverence for monarchy. Sir Tobie had outstanding moral courage and both were brimful of self-confidence. This was especially marked in the younger man when he went out at length alone with his self-reliance and his light talent. The father and son were, I think, attached to one another.

And yet somehow it does not add up. A mere list of qualities is insufficient. Again there has always been to my mind an oppressive character about the whole idea of the Barlow family. It is hard to think of Tobie Mathew as having a real link with that *galère*. The difficulty is emphasized by the fact that at least in its public aspects Sir Tobie's middle age is almost too clear; a rather cruel light beats down upon it. On the other hand we have so little data about his youth or about his life and thoughts before he was twenty-three.

Tobie was elegant and extravagant, but was he passionate? In his account of his conversion there is the general impression that when he was twenty-eight he followed the ordinary course of life that offered to a young bachelor of means. "I frequented plays and worse places." Against the suggestion that he had strong passions may be placed the fact that in his middle life he had become the type of courtier who is safe with women.

This at once brings up the nature of his friendships. I have often wondered about his relations with Francis Bacon, but it is clear that there was here no erotic element. Tobie Mathew was in essence a simple and didactic and at times devout writer. He has a robust reference to Sir Christopher Perkins's boy which he would not have penned had his tastes been similar. Besides, the references to Bacon seem never to grow warmer than friendship. We can indeed say little about Tobie's early adult life except that he was ill and ran into debt and was spoken about and was popular. The impact of Francis Bacon seems to have been the first event that we can measure.

FRANCIS BACON

The name of Francis Bacon has a crucial significance in any reconstruction of Tobie's life. It is not yet clear when they first met, but the association was developed before the autumn of 1601. At that time Bacon was forty; he was neither rich nor successful, but already in a measure isolated. The Essex tragedy was very recent and he had taken a leading part in the prosecution launched by the Crown against his former friend.

Henceforward Tobie Mathew's life was dominated by Bacon's emphasis. Now he was to become the disciple of a great man, who was both solitary and ambitious. In spite of the Jesuit influences, to which later he yielded so completely, Tobie Mathew never lost the unmistakable imprint of Bacon's spirit. This was perhaps reflected in the scepticism with which he came to view the intentions of his contemporaries, and in a certain feeling for pure politics. This last element can be traced in Tobie's very genuine admiration for the Countess of Carlisle.

The association with Bacon developed naturally. There was something eminently satisfactory about the career of Tobie's father, and Bacon quickly gave his confidence to the Bishop of Durham's son. Both men had been born into that world of Elizabethan high official life which could prove so dispiriting to the second generation. Bacon was the youngest child of Queen Elizabeth's first lord keeper and was a nephew of Lady Burghley. It was by this time plain that these connections would be of no service to his career. The Queen was never unaware of Francis Bacon, and he for his part had been brought to see that she would never like or value or even use him.

The debates about Bacon's character which marked the nineteenth-century estimates of his work seem to arise from placing that portentous figure in a narrow setting. If the reading of his character which appeals to me is valid, few men have ever had so great a desire to serve the State. With all his far-flung enquiry he was in many respects insular. When he and Tobie Mathew began their friendship they had both the same experience of travel, a period in France after the University. In Bacon's case this experience was gained in the suite of the Queen's ambassador in Paris nor did he ever seek to enlarge it. He had a deep contentment with the realm of England.

He always stood forth as a defender of Reformation values, but the whole tenor of his life would seem to show that what he defended was Protestantism considered as a political situation and not in any sense as a doctrinal faith. He was without in-

Francis Bacon was the enduring influence in the life of Tobie Mathew, of whom he once spoke as 'another myself'. This woodcut is prefixed to the 1668 edition of the 'Essays'.

terest in and rather repelled by Catholicism, but his opposition to Catholics as such was the result of their hostility to the Elizabethan Settlement. Bacon's own career was founded on the Elizabethan scheme, which he always conceived as essentially political. It would be the duty of any prudent prince to maintain it.

He had a large-minded sympathy for what were then termed the "preciser sort", provided he was not involved in any personal contacts with them. They appeared as a valuable element in a State which would maintain itself in isolation from the Catholic monarchies. Francis Bacon was a devoted son after the fashion of his day, and Lady Bacon had been the learned protectress of all the more reputable Puritan clergy. It was characteristic of Bacon's temperament that he never reacted against any form of thought or belief; on the contrary, he strove to disentangle in each person and idea some elements which would prove of utility to the State. It was only a corollary of such searching appraisal that the residue of usefulness that he discovered in men and notions should have turned out to be so limited.

An element in Bacon's isolation arose from the fact that he must always be the prince's sole adviser. His ideas did not marry with those of his contemporaries. The written word had power with him and alone fully clothed his thought. His projects could be submitted direct to his sovereign or they could be placed before some favourite who it was supposed would then present them. This second method was that which Bacon had hoped to use with the Earl of Essex and was to try a generation later with the Duke of Buckingham.

It seems clear that Bacon saw into men's characters, but could not foresee their actions. He was sharp and perceptive in regard to enmity within his own closed circles, but he did not note the cooling of those who might have been his friends. With King James there was a possibility of success, but Buckingham must have found his thought intimidating. Again, Bacon was wholly alien to that quick martial temperament which was one of the prime assets of both favourites. With all his plumed words he was by nature both cool and unemotional. With this there went one of his many Renaissance legacies: he was perfectly uncensorious. His dislikes were not suffused by any prejudices based upon moral grounds.

It has always seemed to me that the real barrier in the relationship of James I and Francis Bacon was the result of the latter's clear-sighted knowledge of each aspect of the King's affections. King James liked to surround his majesty with a kind of homely and innocent confusion. But out at Gorhambury, reposing in the clement weather on a marble seat above the hornbeam avenue, holding his high-crowned silvered bonnet in his hand, sat Bacon, now Lord Verulam, who knew it all. It was not in him to criticize another's pleasures.

There are elements of unfairness in the way that the charge of flattery is presented. The rich phrasing was in general reserved for the throne and for those whom the sovereign deigned to honour. It is common form to charge Bacon with insincerity in his letters to Robert Cecil, first Earl of Salisbury, for after his death he was ready to attack him. But his cousin died holding the lord treasurer's staff and was therefore a symbol of royal favour. It does not seem accurate to suggest that this was a question of mere self-interest, for Bacon must have been taught by twenty years of scrutiny that he had nothing to hope for from Robert Cecil.

Much, too, must be allowed for the convention of that century. The language of compliment was universal and a letter was not considered well-constructed unless it was both formalized and deferential. With Bacon it was not the style but the content, and very often the implied content, that marked him off from other men. The Machiavellian precepts were shared by Francis Bacon with many of his contemporaries; it was as a perfect royalist in doctrine and in conviction that he stands alone. He placed certain unique values in the juxtaposition of the Crown of England and the English Commonwealth. He matured early and throughout his life would offer to his sovereigns advice and admonition, praise and service.

And yet this is such a difficult period to explore and these last sentences are liable to misinterpretation. These words have all both a Renaissance and what we may call for simplicity a Victorian connotation. There was in Bacon no tendency to any reckless political action. The supreme governor of Bacon's actions was wisdom as a Renaissance statesman would have interpreted that term. He certainly possessed one central weakness: it was not in accordance with the sweep of his large mind to enquire into the attitude towards himself of those who chanced to fall beneath his sliding observation. There was in Bacon's relations with his contemporaries, as in his lack of appreciation of the scientific movements of his time, a certain quality of imprecision. His whole correspondence can be considered as a series of statements and not exchanges; he did not link up. On the side of his personal life this led inevitably to isolation. In his last years he had a concentrated zest for the detail of his Hertfordshire estate, its grots and fountains and Roman statuary. The pleasures of building and lay-out have exercised a recurring appeal to the solitary political figure in English history throughout the centuries of landed property. There is Kitchener's mind turning to each detail of Broome Park. And then Bacon had his immense writings, which no contemporary helped to plan or harness. It has always seemed to me that it was Tobie Mathew's function to mitigate his loneliness.

It is interesting to try to detect the attitude of Tobie's parents towards this friendship. To his father Bacon must have proved quite reassuring. There was in fact much in common in their outlook upon politics. In the Bishop's eyes it would have been to the Queen's Counsel's credit that he had done his duty at Essex's trial. There was no sympathy for that young lord at Durham House. The mother's attitude is much more doubtful; she always had her premonitions.

At the beginning there were solid gains. Tobie had joined Gray's Inn, to which Bacon belonged. On his twenty-fourth birthday he entered the House of Commons as member for the Cornish borough of Newport and in 1604 he changed this seat for St. Albans, which Bacon had made over to him. As a result of these arrangements Tobie was now both a political and literary disciple, and I have sometimes wondered what Bacon hoped to make of him. Perhaps he had thought to employ him gradually in foreign politics, a sphere of government in which he himself had little interest. It is significant that when the old Queen was dying Bacon sent Tobie Mathew as his messenger to deliver a letter to the new sovereign. If this guess is accurate Tobie was very probably the only man whom Bacon ever chose as a political collaborator. The upshot was discouraging enough.

The political relation broke down almost at once. It may have been that Tobie Mathew found too great a similarity between Bacon's ideas and those which his father had for so long expressed to him. The literary discipleship remained, and Tobie would always bear the impress of Bacon's mind. The friendship arranged itself on a new pattern. A phrase in the account of Sir Tobie's conversion can serve as a description of their intimacy in its final stages. "I passed my time with him [Sir Francis] in much gust; for there was not such company in the whole world."

After the changes in his life it was a matter of nearly fourteen years before Tobie was again in England as a free man. There had been constant letters, and the phrasing in one which Bacon sent him in 1609 with a copy of *The Advancement of Learning* is typical of the relationship:

SAGGI MORALI
DEL SIGNORE
FRANCESCO BACONO,
CAVAGLIERO INGLESE,
GRAN CANCELLIERO
D'INGHILTERRA.

Con vn'altro suo Trattato
DELLA SAPIENZA
DEGLI ANTICHI.
Tradotti in Italiano.

IN LONDRA

Appresso di GIOVANNI BILLIO.
1618.

Tobie Mathew was a remarkable linguist. Writing of his stay in Florence, he says 'the language was that mistress which I resolved most to court at that time'. In 1618 *he published in London his Italian translation of Bacon's 'Essays' and 'De Sapientia Veterum'.*

"I have now, at last, taught that child to go, at the swadling whereof you were. My work, touching the Proficiency and Advancement of Learning, I have put into two books, whereof the former, which you saw, I count but a page to the latter. I have now published them both, whereof I thought it a small adventure to send you a copy, who have more right to it than any other man, except Bishop Andrews, who was my inquisitor."

In the following year, 1610, he sent him *De Sapientia Veterum*. The situation had been greatly altered when Tobie returned home again. Sir Francis Bacon had gone through the gradations of solicitor and attorney general, he had been raised to the peerage as Lord Verulam and had attained to the Great Seal. Money had come to him from various sources. He had made a wealthy marriage with Alderman Barnham's child. This had done nothing to check his isolation. His wife's relations, the great silkmen and drapers, did not appeal to him, and her sister was married to the intimately disreputable Lord Castlehaven. The marriage was childless and there is no reason to suppose that Bacon was suited to marital domesticity. He had Gorhambury by now, the statues of the Claudian Emperors, his relaxations. He was isolated in the lord-chancellorship, isolated and unsuspecting. It seems that he felt that he had lulled the House of Commons by those great phrases which never came amiss to him. "But I have spoke", he once told them, "out of the fountain of my heart." He had written to Buckingham in a strain which was quite freed from realism. "I am yours", he had explained,

Cosimo II de' Medici, Grand Duke of Tuscany, reigned at Florence when Tobie Mathew went there in 1605. To him Tobie later dedicated his Italian translation of Bacon's 'Essays'.

PLATE III

Richard Bancroft, Archbishop of Canterbury, did his best to make Tobie change his mind. At their first meeting he 'looked as kindly upon me as that face could tell how to do'.

PLATE IV

"surer to you than my own life. For, as they speak of the turquoise stone in a ring, I will break into twenty pieces before you have the least fall." This is not political writing at all, it is compliment drained of meaning. As the years passed, Lord Verulam gave himself to his large endeavours and especially to the *Novum Organum*, that effort "to bring in estimation, Philosophy or Universality, name and thing".

There were few now to cleave to him. He was a man in great place who could not reward. There was as yet no body of gentlemen interested in enquiries into the natural sciences like that from which Charles II was to form the Royal Society. Had there been, it is doubtful whether Bacon would have made use of them. In the subjects of his study he bent his mind to that enumeration of endless instances that Goethe would describe as *Verulamisch*. Lord Verulam, recently promoted as Viscount St. Albans, was just turned sixty years of age when the catastrophe befell him.

He was never a precisian and was not the man to be careful to depute some cunning fellow to receive his gifts for him. He took the gifts which came to his great place. He was cold at the heart to the equals who pressed about him. In a vague way he always needed money, but his mind was on other matters as he fingered the gifts that parties made to him. Though there was a vein of optimism in much of his writing, he was profoundly sceptical in regard to his contemporaries. It is crucial to an understanding that he seems invariably to have given judgment against those who had offered sums to gain his favour. He was ageing, too, and had so little time. He was cruelly fatigued and Tobie Mathew was a solace to him.

This is how I read the position at the moment when Lord St. Albans was deprived of the Great Seal for taking bribes. He is often accused of weakness in failing to defend himself, but there may have been a certain element of relief that, after all the tempest, his writings and the evolution of his thought could be pursued unhindered. He was freed at last from his own ambition. The fine and imprisonment were remitted through the royal favour. Francis Bacon continued to acknowledge his sovereign's excellence. He was grateful to the King who kept his enemies at bay. For the rest he gave no thought to them. He referred to the "old gold" of the letter that Tobie Mathew wrote to him on his disgrace. They were closer to one another than they had been in earlier days. The Archbishop of York still went forward very mellow and successful. A profound and shared misfortune united Tobie Mathew to his former mentor.

FLORENCE

In the early days of the Italian spring Tobie Mathew first came to Florence. In the autumn of 1604 he had obtained licence from the Government to travel for three years. He had given his parents to understand that he was bound for France and they had agreed to this project, although with hesitation. The Florentine scene was henceforward to have a hold on him.

The view over Florence from San Miniato had at that date taken on the outline which is familar to us, the monuments already weathered in the Tuscan light, the Duomo and its tower and the soft hills. It was by this time an old city with the Ponte Vecchio, the town palaces and churches; but it recalled a past which had no parallel in Northern Europe. All the younger Elizabethan world had been brought up on the story of "Picus Erle of Myrandula". But beyond the early Medicean glory and the possession of that Tuscan speech, which Tobie Mathew so much admired, Florence of the grand dukes had a contemporary significance. It had now become a centre of the formation of those art collections which the seventeenth-century sovereigns would so greatly prize. It was also the home of architectural experiment in the grand manner.

Under another aspect the years of Tobie's visits were those which will be associated with the name of Sustermans. There was perhaps a lack of spontaneity in the social life, and the grand-ducal court itself was formal, spendthrift, rather heavy. The Spanish example held across the length of Italy; there were Spanish viceroys at Milan and Naples. The habits of dress and the approach to religion were deeply influenced by the kings of Spain, that rather sombre dignity of apparel which was one of Philip II's legacies. The portrait of the Grand Duke Cosimo II brings this back: the long Spanish face, perhaps a heritage from the House of Alvarez de Toledo; the cloak of the grand master of Santo Stefano revealing a slashed and embroidered doublet, Spanish breeches and silk stockings, the whole in black. There is a quality of stiffness in the Sustermans portraits which record this generation, the princesses with the embroidered flowers in gold and silver, the delicate formal lace, the ropes of pearls.

Over all there lay the shadow of the Pitti Palace, the massive wings now rising, the gravelled spaces, the terrace and the fountain with the marble cupids, the box and cypresses. Villas and their gardens were now planned as a unit, the double avenue of cypresses and parterres, the whole disposed. The note is perhaps struck by the new care for Florentine inlay and the establishment of the manufactory of *pietra dura*, the mosaic and the hard colours.

This was universally accepted as a period of achievement. It is clear that Tobie Mathew remembered every detail. If it was Francis Bacon who formed much of Tobie's outlook on his contemporaries, it was the Florentine influence that made the courtier.

The gallery of statues at the Uffizi had been completed and the pieces placed upon the marble floor beneath the mother-of-pearl ceilings set in gilded *gesso*. The Medici mausoleum attached to San Lorenzo was then building. The great smooth slabs of porphyry were in place, the coats of arms of the cities of Tuscany inlaid in jasper and agate. The plan for the roof of the dome was set out for perusal; it was to be formed of inset squares of Persian *lapis lazuli*. These details may convey the impression of a rather circumscribed and cold splendour. It was precisely what that generation so much admired.

In this connection it is only necessary to recall the eulogy in the *Reliquiae Wottonianae*. "The Palace of Pitti at Florence", wrote Sir Henry Wotton, "I came often to review, and still methought with fresh admiration; being incomparably (as far as I can yet speak by experience or report) for solid architecture the most magnificent and regular pile within the Christian world." The style of the Pitti Palace would not spread northward except to Munich where Duke Maximilian would soon erect the *Alte Residenz*. On the other hand the creation of galleries of pictures and statuary was to become an absorbing interest at Whitehall. In this Tobie Mathew was a precursor. Charles I would purchase the Duke of Mantua's collections. A man of taste and perception would always make his way to some kind of favour with the Stuart kings.

A phrase in Tobie Mathew's *Conversion* brings back the effect which the city and the still country-side made on him. "For I remember that two of them"—and he is here speaking of gentlemen who were his friends—"were walking once with myself into certain villas to see the manner of the country and to taste their fruits: and by chance we fell into a church, which chanced to be in our way: and it was that of Fiesole."

Another side of Florentine life was to have a deep if transitory effect in England, the formulae for those elaborate masques which gave their special colour to the idea of entertainment. For about this time, in 1608 to be exact, Monteverdi's opera *Ariadne* was first given at Mantua and the masque of *Il Giudizio di Paride* performed at Florence. The mechanical details, but especially the designs of this last masque were to affect English practice for nearly forty years until the outbreak of the Civil Wars. The "preciser sort" would never relish all the cumbrous artifice. This was another subject on which Tobie would develop a certain expert but polite knowledge. In thirty years' time, as he sat, an old man now, watching *Tempe Restored* or the *Queen of Aragon* in the cold northern weather, he would recall the effects they used again, only sometimes less skilfully. There was the garden of Calypso from *Il Giudizio di Paride*, the tall slender columns and perspective, the hanging terraces. Or there was the fleet of Amerigo Vespucci from this same masque, the dolphins and the ships and tritons.

Much of the stock scenes which had delighted his youth were suitable for *Britannia Triumphans*, where the worn palace of fame was refurbished once more. All very old-fashioned, but he was by then a practised courtier.

The account already quoted reveals his interests. "I went equally", Tobie was to write later about this stay in Florence, "to the mountebanks . . . I read also books of all kinds, and very often such as were of the lightest air; as comedies whose matter not affecting the mind much, the words would both come quicklier, and stick closer to it. For the language was that mistress which I resolved most to court at that time." On the political side he was gaining a very solid grounding, all the more valuable because he was not tempted to unconventionality. He had in fact the talents and equipment which would have made a fine career if only he had not become a Catholic.

There are many angles from which the matter of Tobie Mathew's conversion can be approached. The possibility does not seem to have germinated in his mind until some months after he had reached Italy. His own account describes the controversial works to which he was directed, and in particular a book by William Reinolds. The title will sufficiently indicate its nature: *A Refutation of sundry Reprehensions*. Arguments were given to him from the Fathers and passages suggested for his reading. He would sit in the college vineyard after dining with Father Parsons (for it was with the Jesuits that he was in touch), talking about Augustine and Cyprian and Tertullian. Tobie had always had a feeling for St. Augustine, and it has occurred to me that he may have felt that the *Confessions* in some way mirrored his own experience. It may be so.

Two passages from his own writings have always seemed to me to give the clearest impression of Tobie Mathew's frame of mind. "Yet there", he writes in that part of the account of his conversion which deals with his stay in Naples, "I had a certain odd encounter, and it was this: every day there passed once, and sometimes oftener, under my window near a certain hour, a procession of little boys, singing the litanies of our Blessed Lady. And I know not by what chance, or rather Providence of Almighty God, the tune of that sweet verse, *Sancta Maria, Ora pro nobis*, came so often in at mine ears, and contented me so much that at length my tongue took it up; not indeed as a prayer (such was my misfortune at that time; for it is misery to have been, at any time, other than our Blessed Lady's most humble servant) but as a song, whose ditty fell not unpleasingly to that air, and so, when I found myself alone, my usual entertainment would be to sing *Sancta Maria, Ora pro nobis*, in the tune of those babes and sucklings, who showed forth her praise." There is in the phrasing of these ideas something reminiscent of Henry Lawes and a very faint suggestion of Richard Crashaw.

The second passage is wholly different, but is of interest as indicating what were to become Tobie's new rock-like certitudes. "For", he explains in relating his conferences with Fr. Parsons, "the truth and certainty of Catholic doctrine is such that I hold it at this day the greatest miracle of the whole world that a man who is in any way of a judgment and will which is not mightily depraved, can forbear to subscribe entirely to the truth of Catholic doctrine, and to acknowledge his obedience to the holy Catholic Church, upon that kind of conference and proof, which he may easily hear thereof, within the space of a very few hours, from any Catholic learned man." This was always to be his standpoint but one tempered, perhaps, by a wise avoidance of any discussions upon religious questions in a general company.

This was the period of the streaming Catholic life of the Counter-Reformation, the generations dominated by the Council of Trent and hence known as Tridentine. Here was a doctrine which appeared to Tobie Mathew to be based on principles which were both logical and irrefutable. Still it would be a mistake to underestimate the secular appeal of the Catholic presentation in that time and place. This may be best described as the powerful attraction of an integrated society. That factor was emphasized more clearly because Tobie's journeys took place during the twenty years of peace between the signature in 1598 of the Peace of Vervins, which brought to an end the conflict between France and Spain, and the outbreak of the Thirty Years War in 1618. The rivalries of the western monarchies were therefore muted and the double marriage between the children of Philip III and those of Henry IV stressed new bonds. Peace on the grand scale flowered beneath a Rubens heaven.

It was perhaps in the first quarter of the seventeenth century that the politico-religious unity of the Tridentine world seemed most apparent. The background of Catholic faith and practice, stronger than these subsequently became, gave unity to the western structure. Viewed from the Florentine angle England seemed away on the rim of civilization. The desire for unity among the different monarchies exercised a pull upon King James, although he had never travelled. This is apparent in the considerations that he advances when examining the Western Patriarchate in *A Premonition to all Kings of Christendom*. "And for myself (if that were yet the question) I would with all my heart give my consent that the Bishop of Rome should have the first Seat: I being a Western King would go with the Patriarch of the West."

To the Roman mind such considerations were at once inadequate and otiose. There was a mathematical quality in the way in which the Tridentine world would be presented. It was the purpose of those who worked in the perfecting of the Baroque styles to give concrete expression to this triumph. Allegory was much in vogue and history was not neglected. Thus Tobie Mathew was asked to visit the catacombs of St. Sebastian. "I must", he wrote, "confess in the presence of God that the sight of those most ancient crosses, altars, sepulchres, and other marks of the Catholic religion, having been planted there in the persecution of the primitive Church did strike me with a kind of reverent awe." The Catholic position appeared to Tobie Mathew as unassailable. A point is perhaps worth making: it is doubtful how far he understood those who in England were henceforth to be his co-religionists.

One secular element in the Continental scheme of values appealed to him; he had what was almost a reverence for exact station. This is a point which it is hard for the modern generation to appreciate. In the England of that day it had some affinity with Erastian ideas; it was, however, no man's practice. It required the clarity of the Latin mind; it is found in its perfection in Saint-Simon. It was part of a graded courtesy in spiritual and temporal affairs which is reflected in the Spanish temperament. It can be conceived as the recognition, within limits, of each man's worth. Two quotations from Tobie Mathew's writings bear on this point. The first passage occurs after the description of an accident to his mule when he was riding along the road to Naples between Velletri and Sermoneta. "The Bishop of Malta, with divers Cavaliers of that Order passed then in our company, or rather (to speak more properly) we in theirs." The second example is found in an account of Cardinal Pinelli's kindness to him, a stranger. "For the Cardinal would never speak to me till I had put on my hat as soon as he; nor till I sat down in as good a chair as his; and whensoever I parted from him, he accompanied me two or three rooms from his own." I set this down, for it is an element that I have always found a trifle disconcerting. It is not easy to imagine his father the Archbishop using such phrases. At times this has made me feel that perhaps Sir Tobie was humourless. Another way of putting it is this: Tobie Mathew may have considered that anything that touched on courtesy was too grave a matter to be made the subject of a jest.

In March 1606 in the church of the Annunziata at Florence he made his submission at the hands of Fr. Lelio Ptolomei of the Society of Jesus. He now returned to England with such equipment as his journey gave him. One question is not easy to answer. What did he expect to happen when he went back?

In a sense he may have been lulled into a false security by the various English Catholic gentlemen whom he had met upon his travels, like Sir George Petre and Mr. Cansfield. It is worth remarking that both he and they had been abroad during the Gunpowder Plot excitements. They were therefore unaware of the exacerbated temper in political England. Besides, while his friends were prosperous landowners, Tobie had no estate and few resources. He must vacate his seat in Parliament. It is my reading of the situation that Tobie Mathew placed all his hope on gaining access to the King.

There is something unreal about Tobie's next stay in England. He went on arrival to a "private French ordinary at the East end of London near the Tower" and after a few days moved to lodgings in Fleet Street. He wrote at once to Francis Bacon and through him to Lord Salisbury, the secretary of state, asking in effect permission to live peacefully and unmolested. He does not seem to have communicated with his own family. Tobie did, however, call to pay his respects at Lambeth. With Salisbury and Archbishop Bancroft he had approached the chief powers in Church and State. He met everywhere with courtesy and even kindness. The ecclesiastics in particular did their best to free him from the Roman errors. In regard to Bancroft Tobie has a sharp expression. "He thanked me", he stated in an account of his first meeting with the primate, "and embraced me close; and looked as kindly upon me as that face could tell how to do." It must be remembered that Tobie had not really been brought up in episcopal circles.

Very soon the oath of allegiance with its anti-papal implications was proposed to him, and on his refusal he was lodged in the Fleet prison. "The Plague was then hott in London", he wrote afterwards in his *Conversion*, "and yet it was in no power of mine to get released from that prison." He actually remained there for ten months.

Here visitors came frequently, the literary and political figures whom he had known through Bacon, Sir Henry Goodyere and Sir Edwin Sandys and John Donne. His characterization of William Crashaw, the poet's father, is decidedly unfriendly. "For there is not a more intolerable kind of man than the ignorant, audacious, loud and false undertaker, and such he ever was." All the time there is the impression that Tobie was trying to get to the King and that there was a net about him.

There was one man who seemed to aid him in his desire, and who alone had the power, Robert Earl of Salisbury. Tobie Mathew describes his kindness. "During all the time of my imprisonment, this great and gallant man", he writes of this high officer of State, "would needs be putting daily favours upon me, sometimes by giving me lights concerning mine own condition, sometimes by way of advice how to carry myself in order to my addresses and estate; and besides out of his great desire to obtain me some little part of the King's favour, he was earnest with me to write him some letter which might be monstrable by him to the King." After a little study the meaning penetrates to us through the archaic phrasing. And then the question presents itself, what did Lord Salisbury hope to gain by his forbearance?

This minister had never had any tenderness for the faith of the Church of Rome or its professors. A clear mind guided all his actions in that sphere of politics to which he had been born and to which he gave himself completely. Literary projects were outside his scope and he did not like his cousin Francis Bacon. Before the journey to Florence he had shown himself unfriendly rather than otherwise to Tobie Mathew. On the other hand, like his father Lord Burghley, he appreciated the Archbishop of York. Both these statesmen realized that Tobie's father was no mere fair-weather friend to the royal authority. But this last motive was surely insufficient to sway his reason.

Under one aspect Salisbury may be regarded as in essence a talent scout; he sought constantly, and of course within prescribed limits, for recruits to the King's service. And Tobie Mathew had many of the qualities that in time would make an envoy. There was much opportunity in this employment, then in embryo. It was necessary to modify a single point which would disqualify him, and Salisbury, with so much else to do, set out to clear up the situation. There is reason to suppose that forbearance was a weapon which he liked to use. All that

Robert Cecil, Earl of Salisbury, 'this great and gallant man' (as Tobie Mathew called him) showed much kindness to Tobie while he was lodged in prison.

was needed was to tarnish Tobie's Catholic allegiance, to induce him to some step which would destroy the confidence that the Court of Rome might otherwise place in him to the King's detriment. Once his reputation as a Catholic was bruised, he might prove a useful representative at foreign courts. It was no disadvantage that his position in regard to religious matters might be in some respects equivocal. This may seem elaborate, but I can find no other reading which can explain the harassed minister's long patience.

Tobie's father now began to act, but with much more directness. His intention at any rate is clear: it was to dissipate his son's young follies. It is worth pausing on his two emissaries. "There came to me also one Mr. Cooper, who was a practiser and counsellor at law; and he held also a kind of office under my father. This man would still be telling me how the law of England stood at this day, and what mighty dangers a man incurred by taking those unlawful courses wherein I was." The second visitor was a character of more importance. "Doctor Albericus Gentile, the Doctor of the chair in Oxford for Civil Law," explains Tobie in his account, ". . . gave me several visits . . . he was employed to use some diligences by my father." It is in this connection that there occurs a very celebrated passage. The two men were speaking of the oath of allegiance. "He [Dr. Gentili] said I should do discreetly to take it in such sort as he had taken his oath of believing the Council of Trent before he came out of Italy in his youth. I asked him how that was; and he made me this answer in direct words (for we spoke

TOP: *King James I, who exiled Tobie in 1605 and knighted him in 1623.* LEFT: *George Villiers, first Duke of Buckingham, favourite of James I and Charles I.* BOTTOM: *John Donne, the poet, knew Tobie well and visited him in prison.*

PLATE V

Thomas Howard, second Earl of Arundel and Surrey, was a famous art collector and travelled much on the Continent.

PLATE VI

Italian): '*Giusto come pigliarei un scudello di brodetto*'— Just as I would take a mess of broth."

There were further conversations and a lengthy interview with Lancelot Andrewes, Bishop of Chichester, for whom Tobie had a great respect. Neither side gained their point, for Tobie did not yield and the King remained invisible. Eventually, and perhaps on Bacon's advice, the royal permission was sought and obtained for another foreign journey. "I was advised", Tobie Mathew's account explains, "by some friends rather to retire myself handsomely out of the way, for the safety of the poor fortune which I enjoyed, than still to be shut up in prison. . . . I gave way to be so disposed of, and though I went over with a fair licence, yet I was directed in mine ear not to return, till the King's further pleasure was first known." He repaired abroad to the Court of Brussels. He was thirty-one years of age and was back in those States which were the appanages of the Spanish monarchy. Tobie Mathew was middle-aged when he returned to England, and it is as a courtier in middle life that he is painted. There is no doubt that he was in some ways an inscrutable young man.

THE RUBENS PERIOD

The ten years that followed must have been the most difficult of Tobie Mathew's life. He had little security and only a vague hope of returning to England. The desire to return grew steadily stronger, and there was no scope for his talent. His financial situation was precarious; there seem few grounds for John Donne's optimistic rumour that in 1612 Tobie already had a fortune of £7,000. It was difficult for exiles in the opulent Netherlands.

Tobie's relations with his own country were governed by his contacts with the English envoys who entertained him, endeavoured to make use of him and reported on all his actions. It is clear that both Sir Dudley Carleton and Sir Henry Wotton, who were continuously and alternately envoys at Venice and the Hague from the beginning of Tobie's exile until the end of King James's reign, were determined to make it plain in London that they had no sympathy with this guest. It would seem that Carleton was at heart his friend and as cordial as it was safe to be; Wotton on the other hand disliked him. Perhaps this was because Wotton disliked his serious acceptance of the Baroque world.

Tobie Mathew had indeed now come to the scene of its full northern splendour. Rubens, who was barely four months his senior, had just returned to Antwerp from his years at Rome and Mantua as one of Duke Vincenzo's painters. He had already decorated the chapel of St. Helen in Santa Croce in Gerusalemme, the church which had given Archduke Albert his cardinalitial title. It was the season of that Jesuit architecture which was allied with the obvious taste for spectacle and *décor* now alive in the Southern Netherlands. In the homeland of *La Kermesse Héroïque* the striking tableaux of the saints may be considered a religious conterpart to every form of secular display. This was a period in which a renewed material prosperity had given to the life of the Low Countries an air that was convincing and also suggested opulence. In some ways this could be envisaged as the Tridentine scene in its more bourgeois aspect. The court was chaste, the archduchess serious and devout and the archduke a Hapsburg cardinal of profound respectability. There was the spirit of the *joyeuse entrée*, rich costume and a lavish hospitality, a not too formal dignity. For recreation they had the madrigals composed by Peter Philips, one of the organists of the archdukes' chapel. The sovereigns were childless; their entourage was sedate; there was a hint of prudery. Brussels was not a capital that Tobie favoured. His feeling was for the South with its subtleties and gradations. There is small reason to suppose that he was drawn to Rubens's literalness or to his obvious and sun-flecked cogency.

Nevertheless it is with Rubens that Tobie Mathew's name is linked. It seems that his approach to the painter's work was not so much through his art as through that religious expression with which both men had sympathies. He was impressed, but how far was he attracted? Now year by year the great canvases at Antwerp were hoisted into place, the "Adoration of the Kings" for the municipality, the "Descent from the Cross" at Notre Dame, the "Mystic Espousals of St. Rosalia" at Saint-Paul, the "Return from Egypt" at Saint-Charles, and the three large altar pieces in the same Jesuit church; all these works in the one city and, as a modern touch, the "Miracles of St. Francis Xavier".

It is worth pausing to consider how such works were regarded by those whose somewhat dilettante taste would concentrate later upon Van Dyck. There was a delicate, almost feminine, quality in this latter portrait painter's work which courtiers in time would come to prize. On the other hand it seems doubtful whether the crowded scenes commissioned by Marie de Médicis for the gallery of the Hôtel de Luxembourg appealed to the then English taste; the amber creamy torsos which Rubens loved and the helmets like dilapidated Alexanders. It was a matter of instinct and not of knowledge, perhaps also of prejudice.

In Tobie's case we can form a judgment from two letters which were the result of his efforts to assist his friends in England to make the purchases which they desired. It should be explained that he found himself engaged in negotiations undertaken in the first place by Sir Dudley Carleton. The question

Sir Dudley Carleton, later created Viscount Dorchester, one of the most successful diplomatists of his time. Tobie Mathew corresponded with him about the purchase of Rubens pictures. While he was staying in Venice in 1610, Carleton was appointed English Envoy there.

arises as to whether Tobie Mathew was interested in pictures at all or only ready to use his knowledge of the world and to give pleasure. The evidence now before us has always made me hesitate.

It should be explained that in these commercial transactions a difficulty was created by the degree to which the painter was assisted by the other workers in his studio. The first letter relates to the "Fox and Wolf Hunt" which was finally sold to the Duke of Aerschot. Tobie Mathew is found explaining to Carleton that Rubens is making another but smaller picture of the same subject "for the gusto which he takes in that peece of hunting. His later picture if you like to have you may; and he undertakes to make it of as much perfection as the other, if not more." The next letter addressed to Lord Danvers and relating to the "Lion and Tiger Hunt", the original being purchased for the Duke of Bavaria's gallery at Munich, deals with the same subject in sharper terms. "Rubens confesseth in confidence", he wrote, "that this is not all of his owne doinge and now I thanke him for this confession, for a man who hath but halfe an eye, may easily discerne it: but he protests that he has touched it over all, in all the partes of it. I must confess as a truth to your Lordship (though I know he will be angry at it, if he know it), that it scarce doth looke like a thinge that is finished and the colorito of it doth little please me, though upon the whole manner it be a gallant peece, for the desseigne of it is precious." To me it is doubtful if Tobie really had any care at all for the "gallant peece". Such services might help to pave the way for his return.

It is difficult to work out the chronology of his forced travels, but it seems that he went to Madrid for a period and then back again to Brussels. There were many contacts with the English. Lord Arundel came to Louvain at this time. The parties travelling to the "Spaw" and to Germany increased, and among the latter came Sir Robert Drury with John Donne in his train. Donne in this winter of 1611–12, although just on forty, was still without security, travelling at the expense of a new patron. Mrs. Donne was at home, living in the same patron's mansion, Drury House, with all the children. These facts are mentioned to underline the sensitiveness of Donne's approach to his old acquaintance. The account is interesting as providing one of the few glimpses of Tobie Mathew that have survived from these dark years.

"You have lost again", wrote Donne in reporting a rumour of Tobie's death, "a very worthy friend, who had so much worthiness to be lost all at once; a gentleman, whom, in good faith, I ever loved well, out of those things which were within my comprehension which were his wit and appliableness; but, since his death, I hear of an exercise of his judgment, which I knew not before which is that he loved not me. This is Mr. Mathew." The letter then goes on to other statements whose accuracy we are unable to control. "He [Tobie Mathew] is said to have given all his estate to Mr. Gage, and that is said to be £7,000, which gentleman hath since lost one of his eyes, which I mention as a loss of which I am sensible and compassionate." Who was this Mr. Gage?

George Gage was to prove a lifelong intimate. He was a cadet of that Recusant family whose home was at Firle Place under the Sussex Downs; his younger brother Sir Henry would be governor of Oxford in the Civil Wars. It is difficult to piece his history together. He was certainly five and probably ten years younger than Tobie Mathew. He had been educated in Flanders; Tobie seems to have taught him and made him. He was to be for some time his constant companion. By the summer of 1612 they had gone together into Italy. "Here are newly arrived", we read in a note of strangers come to Venice, "Toby Mathew and his comrade Mr. Gage by Basil and Milan."

It is clear that by this time the sense of exile had deepened, and Venice was not a city in which he could find himself at ease. The quarrel with the Papacy was not long over; there was an admiration for the capitalist ventures of the Elizabethan Age; there was the intermittent presence of an English envoy who was hardly prepared to extend those courtesies by which the exiles set so much store. Tobie Mathew had known Sir Henry Wotton all through his adult life. He was familiar with the poet's temperament, the imprudence and the soft masked jealousy.

There was little welcome for Tobie Mathew at the English embassy in Cannaregio near the Ponte degli Ormesani while Wotton sat there with his friends in the green velvet arm chairs beneath the walls with the gilded leather. It is a scene that we can reconstruct exactly: the furniture hired from Venetian Jews, the carpets spread upon the heavy tables, the Titians subject to resale. In the evenings Wotton played upon the *viola da gamba*; he was getting a trifle elderly, an old-fashioned fantastic. Beside him a favourite ape toyed with his chain. He sent rose cuttings and melon seed to the King; he was very serviceable but cautious. He would recommend the singing of the nuns at San Girolamo, but he was careful to keep clear of Catholic exiles. In the hot weather he retired to his villa on the canal of the Brenta where he played bowls on the greensward and in September pressed his grapes. He sent little presents, Parmesan cheese and olives, Murano glasses. Wotton was proud of his Italian and valued his association with Francis Bacon. Possibly he was jealous of Tobie on both these points. He had the great man's interest in science, polite and rudimentary; he studied the cutting of the softer gems. In some ways he did not outgrow the atmosphere of Euphuism in which he had been bred at Essex House. He was dangerous, questing and under certain aspects effeminate. The element of the precious never left him. "This week", he wrote once to a friend, "we have been visited by dolphins of extraordinary greatness from the sea, playing in the canal of Giudecca."

In the year that Tobie first came to Venice Lord Salisbury died. He had not redeemed his promise; but to the end of his life Tobie Mathew spoke well of him. There was no link with the King's new favourite Robert Carr, who first became Viscount Rochester and then Earl of Somerset. Lord Arundel, whom Tobie had met in Louvain, now reappeared. He was moving slowly down Italy, and Inigo Jones was travelling at his expense. Tobie Mathew and George Gage had reached Rome, and an acquaintanceship was formed with Thomas Coke, who made Lord Arundel's purchases. The tone of this period is set in a letter from Tobie to Coke, the latter then staying at Naples. "If I can recover a little health, I think to go into a villa for the taking of some fresh air. If in the meantime you return this letter will meet with you, and also a roll of pictures I have left for Don Roberto."

Carleton had now replaced Wotton as envoy at Venice and Tobie was brought, at least by correspondence, into his circle. The acquistion of *objets d'art* for England was pressed forward, works by Veronese and "old Bassan" and Tintoretto's "Queen of Sheba". There were many statues, including heads of Brutus and Germanicus. It was weary waiting with a "roll of pictures for Don Roberto". Tobie Mathew was nearing forty. Carleton was wary, ready to meet him on the neutral ground of art collections but clearly unprepared to make a positive recommendation in his favour. It was Carleton's duty to his own career to hold the scales.

Tobie Mathew then tried Lord Arundel. The two men were mere acquaintances, and Arundel kept an almost royal state. There were many factors tending to make them mutually antipathetic. The Earl was passing away from the Church which Tobie had joined and for which he suffered. Moreover he had a technical interest in pictures and in statuary; he was perhaps the one patron from England who genuinely appreciated Rubens. This was in contrast with what would seem to have been

Tobie's good-humoured taste and readiness to judge a nice perspective. On the other hand Arundel had a complete lack of interest in those political situations which had become for Tobie Mathew a main preoccupation. Finally it was one of the Earl's settled maxims never to seek a favour from either of his sovereigns. The actual return to England came about through a very different intermediary.

It has always interested me to notice that although Tobie Mathew was a Catholic and indeed, as will appear, a priest, the assistance that he needed in time of trouble came from those who had no sympathy for his religious faith. In this case his first return was compassed by the King's new favourite; nor is this surprising, for in the early days of his ascendancy the Marquess of Buckingham was prodigal of his favours and took pleasure in doing good. The account of this change of fortune is given by Tobie Mathew. "And having about the end of that time", he wrote in the description of his conversion, "made an acquaintance in France with Mr. Villiers, who grew afterwards to be the King's favourite and Duke of Buckingham; and he, remembering, when he was come home, the civilities which had passed between him and me at Paris, and how it had been my fortune to bid him return quickly into England, and to bespeak him, and to tell him, that he should prove the favourite of the time (which he published afterwards to all the world), he resolved to press King James that he would permit me to return into my country." There are certain inaccuracies to be noted. The contact with George Villiers cannot be placed later than 1613, the year in which the future favourite returned from France at the age of twenty-one. Tobie Mathew did not land in England until May 1617. It is clear that someone must have assisted Lord Buckingham's memory. There seems every reason to suppose that Tobie's benefactor was Francis Bacon.

It is worth touching on this matter, for the relation between Buckingham and Tobie was to prove both difficult and impermanent. In this it perhaps mirrored the ill-ease that the favourite displayed whenever he turned his mind towards Lord Verulam. In the days of his great power the Duke was able to secure the promotion of all men whom he really favoured. As a corollary it is fair to assume that those of his intimate acquaintance who did not receive employments had failed to gain his sympathy. The correspondence between them that survives suggests that Buckingham was amused by Tobie Mathew and taken, perhaps, by his linguistic talent. It was in this favourite's nature to appreciate accomplishments. On the other hand he was of a sanguine temper and during his first years unsuspecting. Any refinement of thought he greatly feared. In particular he was burdened by those processes which Lord Verulam revealed to him. That mentor's description of Tobie Mathew in a letter written to the Duke was not encouraging. "Mr. Mathew, a gentleman much your Lordship's servant and to me another myself." The term "another myself" could not fail to strike a chill in the mind of a man of pleasure who was already sufficiently embarrassed by Lord Verulam's imaginings. Be this as it may, the Marquess of Buckingham's first intervention in Tobie's affairs was purely casual.

The whole of Tobie Mathew's next stay in his own country, which lasted from May 1617 until January 1619, was shadowed by the fact that the terms of his return were not made clear. Buckingham had given the first careless impulse, he did no more. In any case he was always cheerful and insensitive in regard to any point which touched upon religious matters. He forced his young wife into Anglican conformity, nor was his confessor Dr. Laud the man to move him towards leniency. Moreover it was a secret of his success that in his early days he never pressed the King in anything. And King James had shown a preference—for one cannot put the position too strongly in the case of a sovereign who in this matter was so personal—remitting and insisting, as the mood took him, that Tobie Mathew's return should be linked with his acceptance of the oath of allegiance.

In consequence Tobie lived more or less in retirement, staying with Lord Verulam at Gorhambury and keeping his own apartment in London. There is a letter of the period from John Donne to Tobie which shows them to be still in friendship: "There is a dangerous rule in law, socius socii mei non est socius meus. If it extend to friendship as well as to familiarity, I, who can pretend no other title to your friendship than that I am allowed some little interest in them, who have more in you, may well account myself to be within the danger of it. But, as in divine, so in moral things, where the beginning is from others, the assistance and co-operation is in ourselves. I, therefore, who could do nothing towards the begetting, would fain do somewhat towards the breeding and cherishing of such degrees of friendship as formerly I had the honour to hold with you. . . . That we differ in our ways, I hope we pardon one another. Men go to China both by the Straits and by the Cape. I never misinterpreted your way, nor suffered it to be so, wheresoever I found it, in discourse. For I was sure you took not up your Religion upon trust, but paid ready money for it, and at a high rate. And this taste of mine towards you, makes me hope for, and claim the same disposition in you towards me."

This and the succeeding years were the period of Tobie's literary work. He issued an Italian translation of Bacon's *Essays* provided with a dedication to the Grand Duke of Tuscany which enabled him to compose an eulogy of Bacon's genius. He also began his best-known work, a translation of the *Confessions of St. Augustine*. He made fairly frequent and perhaps too private visits to the Spanish ambassador, Count Gondomar. The Spanish Marriage—under which comprehensive term may be grouped the various projects for the marriages of King James's two sons with the King of Spain's two daughters—was always unpopular in England. It was at this time that the attention of the writers of news-letters and the pamphleteers was first drawn to Tobie Mathew. Once they were on his track they would never leave him. He was unable to satisfy the King in the matter of the oath of allegiance, and the position became increasingly difficult. After

THE

CONFESSIONS

OF THE

INCOMPARABLE

DOCTOVR

S. AVGVSTINE,

Tranſlated into Engliſh.

TOGEATHER

With a large Preface, which it will much import to be read ouer firſt; that ſo the Booke it ſelfe may both profit, and pleaſe, the Reader, more.

Cibus ſum grandium, creſce, & manducabis me.

D. Aug. Conſ. l. 7. c. 10.

I am the food of ſtrong perſons; grow vp, and thou ſhalt be able to eate me &c.

Permiſſu Superiorum. M.DC.XX.

This first English translation of St. Augustine's 'Confessions', printed at St. Omer in 1620, is Tobie Mathew's best-known literary work. He may have felt that the 'Confessions' in some way mirrored his own experience.

eighteen months it was signified to him that it was the royal pleasure that he should go abroad. "I was fain", he wrote, "to retire myself once again beyond the seas."

This second period of exile was in every respect happier. "It is true", wrote Tobie in regard to this time, "that my temporal means was lessened . . . but yet still, that which was left was abundant, and afterwards my parents themselves gave also good supplies." He seems to have passed the greater part of the next two years in Brussels. It was now evident that one day he would come back to England; only the actual circumstances remained in doubt.

The means of his return were in fact this same Spanish Marriage. "Within one year after this", Tobie explains, "the times grew a little more easy, and a noble, and effectual real friend and favourer of mine, My Lord of Bristol, had both so much good will and so much power, as to obtain my absolute return home." It is curious to watch how this occurred.

It has always appeared to me that the explanation of Tobie's life lies in the fact that his real talent was for diplomacy. And Lord Bristol was the man who believed in the Spanish Marriage: not that he seems to have considered it desirable, but that he looked on it as a matter of settled policy whose details it was his own duty to solve. He was a man who had been close enough to the King's favour to be advanced by it without incurring the jealousy of those who subsequently became the real favourites. In the course of his twelve years as ambassador in Madrid he received his earldom and a privy-councillorship

Lucy Hay, Countess of Carlisle, a daughter of the ninth Earl of Northumberland. All the poets of the time celebrated her beauty and her wit. A brilliant figure at the Court of Charles I, she was for many years a power in politics. Tobie Mathew's 'Character of the Countess' is known to have circulated in manuscript in 1636; it was printed in 1660.

PLATE VII

Endymion Porter, a protégé of Buckingham, became groom of the bedchamber to the Prince of Wales. He had been brought up in Spain and knew the country and the language. In 1623 he accompanied Prince Charles and Buckingham to Madrid; Tobie Mathew was sent out later to advise them.

PLATE VIII

and Raleigh's great sequestrated estate at Sherborne. No other envoy had this strong position. It appears that Bristol valued Tobie Mathew, with whom he had had considerable intercourse in the Low Countries, for his intricate and sympathetic knowledge of Spanish policy and for the ease with which he could read the Latin mind. He was also convinced that he was devoted to the interests of his own sovereign.

One example will serve to throw a light on Bristol's outlook. Thus he understood very clearly King James's desire to recover the Palatinate for his son-in-law, who had lost his inheritance to the Spaniards and Bavarians. But to secure this, Bristol was prepared to go farther than his own Court, since he was ready to concede that the heir to this Calvinist electoral house should be educated in Vienna. He was unconcerned about religious differ ences; it was dynastic preservation that was his aim.

To achieve the Spanish Marriage, Bristol would take any steps that his sovereign suggested to him. He would make plans to fit any instructions, and in Tobie he saw a most unusual instrument. It is clear that the ambassador's outlook was very different from that of either Bacon or Tobie Mathew, but both men would understand him. He belonged to the same order of being. And, if his fortune should be made, he would secure the future of an intimate *protégé*. Upon these terms the King consented. Tobie Mathew would be used in Spain and his religious life left unmolested. On 29 December 1621 he landed again at Dover to begin his career as a diplomat and courtier. He was forty-four; it was the climax of his good fortune.

Tobie Mathew had now come home and for the next twenty years a sharp light would fall on him. His parents were still living; the Archbishop was seventy-five; "his age was then very great, and his interests sat close upon him." Lord St. Albans was working at Gorhambury in enforced retirement. Meanwhile the plans for Tobie's employment in Madrid were going forward; but before they had been completed, the journey to the Court of Spain made incognito by Prince Charles and the Duke of Buckingham, attended only by Sir Francis Cottington and Endymion Porter, had broken in upon a careful diplomatic situation. Shortly after their arrival Tobie Mathew was hastened out. It was at this point that Lord Bristol made the error which broke his own career and frustrated that of his *protégé*.

To a cool and practised mind it seemed incredible that the Prince of Wales would make the journey unless he had determined to conclude the marriage with the Infanta. Otherwise he surely would avoid compromising his dignity. That he was anxious for the restoration of the Palatinate to his sister and brother-in-law was evident enough, and Bristol was convinced that he must have come prepared to make concessions in religion. He was to pay for assumptions which were more suited to the accommodating and serene temper of the eighteenth century. In the then posture of events, and considering that he must assist his sovereign's views, the ambassador enquired whether the Prince of Wales intended to become a Catholic, for this was the opinion held by the people of Madrid. Afterwards, when the journey had proved a complete fiasco and Buckingham and the Prince had returned to England determined to break off the marriage contract, this query was used to bring about Lord Bristol's downfall. No employment was henceforward offered to his *protégé*. In October 1623 Tobie Mathew was knighted by the King at Royston. "For what services", wrote John Chamberlain, "God knows."

This is the moment to consider Tobie's assets and disadvantages as he embarked on his life as a courtier. And to begin with the drawbacks, he seems by this time to have been a priest. This is a matter that has not been, and perhaps cannot be, fully studied. It is commonly asserted that he was ordained a priest together with George Gage by Cardinal Bellarmine at Rome in 1614. Should this fact be accurate, it is not possible to determine how far it was known. Several questions at once arise. Was Tobie accustomed to say Mass; and if so, when and under what conditions? The whole tenor of his life would make it seem improbable that he said

Mass either in London or in Madrid during King James's reign, and it has occurred to me that he may in fact have been ordained much later. Perhaps both he and George Gage, who was employed by the King on an unofficial mission to the Roman Court concerning the marriage with the Infanta, may only have received from Bellarmine those minor orders which would suffice for entry into that clerical body which furnished the Holy See with its trained servants. There is some reason to suppose that George Gage was a priest at least before 1627, when he acted as agent for the seminary at Douai. That Tobie Mathew was a priest at any date after 1630 would appear quite probable, and he was certainly ordained by 1640. But if he only became a cleric in minor orders in 1614, there is apparently no record of his ordination. The whole matter is a minor problem and not yet solved.

Even in his own time there was some mystery. The notion of lay Jesuits was much in the public mind and Tobie suffered through this association of ideas. He was certainly attached to the Society of Jesus, although not a member. Like so many others who have gained their first knowledge of the Church through the Jesuits, he remained convinced throughout life that their standpoint was alone central to the Catholic position. Their lines of thought had for him a logical quality and a supreme coherence. He was sharply impatient of all those who were opposed to them. In the struggle between seculars and regulars his choice was made. In the confused world of the English Catholics he became one of the leading opponents of the Bishop of

Chalcedon who, as he conceived it, denied to the Jesuits that freedom of action which they required.

It was inevitable that such a standpoint should serve to isolate him from a great body of the Catholic gentry. It also brought about a gradual separation from George Gage, who as late as 1622 had been described by watchful onlookers as "Mr. Mathew's *Fidus Achates*". Eventually Gage passed out of Tobie's circle and joined that group of priests who lived in Catholic manor houses. The name appears again in a list of the household of Frances, Countess of Shrewsbury: "my ghostlie father, my cosin Gage". But if his partisan feeling estranged Tobie from many English Catholics, it was also not without its disadvantages in wider circles. It is worth noting the extent to which the idea of a Jesuit aroused repugnance.

By this date the phantom of a Jesuit in disguise had taken hold of the imagination. Two brief quotations will make this clear. The first is from *The Foot out of the Snare*, a work by John Gee published in 1624. "If about Bloomsbury or Holborne", wrote the Rev. Mr. Gee, who as a former Catholic claimed a personal knowledge of what he was describing, "thou meet a good smug fellow in a gold-laced suit, a cloak lined thorow with velvet, one that hath good store of coin in his purse, rings on his fingers, a watch in his pocket, which he will value at twenty pounds, a very broad laced band, a stiletto by his side, a man at his heels, willing (upon small acquaintance) to intrude himself into thy company, and still desiring further to insinuate with thee; then take heede of a Jesuite of the prouder sort of priests." Another variant occurs in a note sent two years later to the secretary of state by the first Viscount Falkland, then lord deputy in Ireland. "An old Jesuit somewhat inclined to grossness, of a sanguine complexion but a sour countenance, his habit of the Spanish fashion, but cloak, doublet and hose being of a sad mixed coloured cloth." He asked that this character should be apprehended. It is significant how closely the official letter tallies with the wording of the pamphleteer. Through Tobie's life this was to be the common mood.

A final disadvantage lay in the Spanish affiliations. Once the negotiations in Madrid were broken off, any connection with them created prejudice. Besides, the fact of a French marriage had succeeded to the project of a Spanish marriage. In 1625 James I died and his son brought back a French princess. Sir Tobie Mathew had to make his way with Charles I and Henrietta Maria as his new sovereigns.

On the other hand he had marked assets. To achieve his aim he was assisted by an intimate, even a recondite, knowledge of the practice of the courts of the Tridentine tradition. His talent for limning in words the character of a princess was unique. His descriptions—what were then called his pictures—of the Infanta Maria and of the Queen were unrivalled in their delicacy of touch, which was at once urbane and respectful. They had something of that classical mould which the Society of Jesus cultivated; they were praise-laden and serene and wholly unexceptionable. In these years Sir Tobie was in his fifties and he made a great appeal to women of a swift intelligence. The Queen was a mere child, too young for him, a disparity of more than thirty years. It was Lady Carlisle who would appreciate that purposeful and elaborate wit, backed by his knowledge. He had to come to the Queen filtered through Lucy Countess of Carlisle and the Duchesse de Chevreuse.

He had the formal literary graces, the verbal felicities, but so much more. A comparison with the Jesuit Jakob Balde will make this clear. That priest was then teaching at Ingolstadt and the elegies that he would write when court preacher at Pfalz-Neuburg drew in verse upon the same conventions as Tobie's prose. A quotation from the *Chorea Mortualis* composed on the death of the young Empress Leopoldina will bear this out.

Ergo vale, o Leopoldina,
Nunc umbra, sed olim regina;
Vale, tibi nil nocuit sors,
Vale, vale, nam profuit mors.

This was the incense which the Baroque world would offer to the faithful sovereigns. It was not ungrateful to the thought of Cardinal Bellarmine:

Bella super et Suecica castra.

Here was one of Tobie Mathew's themes. He bent his mind to the designs of the Cardinal de Richelieu and the King of Sweden; he liked to see the pieces moved. There is something of permanent value in his "Character of the Countess of Carlisle". True, there is the substratum of conventional elegance, those formal rules which then gave so much pleasure; but beyond, there was the play of unobstructed intelligence.

It is interesting to consider the bond between them. Two sentences from Tobie's "Character" may throw some light on this. "Her wit being most eminent among the rest of her great abilities, she affects the conversation of the persons who are most famed for it. . . . She cannot love in earnest so contenting herself to play with love as with a child. Naturally she hath no passion at all." It seems that Lady Carlisle admired above all the possession of a political mind and courage. The two great men to whose fortunes she was successively attached, Strafford and Pym, had in their very different fashions both these qualities. Tobie Mathew, too, was notable for his courage through all these gruelling years; he had an undeviating persistence that in itself was memorable.

There were other links with this last patroness. He liked to plot the course and study; it seems to me that essentially he loved the *politiques*, those adepts of statecraft for whom a political equipoise was itself an end. Certainly he had no use for the stupid heavy woman, however devoted to the Society of Jesus; he clearly never took to the favourite's mother, old Lady Buckingham. He turned to Lady Carlisle with her probing mind that bent itself to combinations. At a guess he had a sort of swift and prudent kindness which would have warmed Madame de Sévigné. There was also a reminiscence of Castiglione and of the Court of Urbino in his outlook. To recreate himself he carried on political conversation with all who would engage him.

There were of course the men whom he repelled. He had adopted in his literary works the billowing imagery of Latin Europe. In his preface to the English translation of the *Penitent Bandito* there is a concept which recalls natural history as St. Francis de Sales conceived that study. "I will not", wrote Tobie, "therefore touch that flower, for fear of striking off the dew every drop whereof is a pearl." This also looks forward towards Richard Crashaw's images. Two references to St. Augustine, both in Tobie Mathew's preface to his translation of the *Confessions*, will serve to complete the picture. In the first St. Augustine is seen approaching his bishopric: "At the end of those three years, being drawn to Hippo by a Principall Cavalier, who offered to depend upon his advice, in the way of the spirit & of serving God exactly." This is contemporary in its manner and has as profound a disregard for the changes wrought by history as anything that Bacon ever wrote. With Tobie one cannot escape from this Baroque modernity. In the second passage we have a further sun-warmed parallel. "And it seemes, he was expressly ordeyned for the destruction of that heretyke [Pelagius]; since upon the very day where on that Cocatrice's egg was hatched in England, this Phenix rose from the spicy bed of St. Monica's blessed wombe in Afrike." Such phrases would not commend him to the graver counsellors.

In other quarters the exactness of his courtesy made an appeal. His was the mode of the Pitti

Palace, of Brussels and of Madrid, which he alone had absorbed. No other courtier had this mastery. A passage in the preface to the *Penitent Bandito* set out the aim he set himself. "No thought of death had any power to take . . . so much as the least *puntillio* from the civil respects and compliments, which are used among persons of his nation and condition." All those who had a feeling for the southern courts would turn to him.

These details should suffice to explain the central fact of King Charles's coldness. That sovereign in his private hours was a man of taste who wished to set a fashion which was delicate and yet touched by austerity. He was not attracted by modern southern models. He would purchase extensively but had a preference for the classical and the exact, perhaps even for the fragile. The element of the sensuous was distasteful to him. His personal relations, when once he left behind his hampering shyness, were all marked by simplicity. It is doubtful how much the masque appealed to him; it was the entertainment of his day and he always wished to content Queen Henrietta. The grave side of Van Dyck's portraiture seems to mirror the fashion in which King Charles saw his court.

Besides, in Tobie Mathew's case there was the crucial matter of religion. The King's Anglican sentiments were linked with a distaste for all the Roman apparatus. This distaste was in part masked by the respect which he always showed for the Queen's practices and by his understanding of those English peers who were hereditary defenders of the Old Religion. In addition to his natural reserve

When Charles I, as Prince of Wales, went to Madrid in 1623 to negotiate his marriage to the Infanta, Tobie Mathew was attached to his suite.

he had schooled himself in the fair-weather years to conceal his preferences and his dislikes, the latter sometimes mild and sometimes bitter. The influence of Archbishop Laud, as the primate not as an individual, was very potent with his royal master. The King knew that it was his duty to maintain the Anglican citadel; in his heart he never forgave a man who had deserted from the Church of England. Under the circumstances it is not surprising that Tobie should have turned towards the *politiques*.

As far as the House of Stuart was concerned, the real link would have been with James I, if only Tobie could have penetrated to the King's sometimes bemused but always active mind with its detailed, almost scholarly, concern for all that pertained to sovereignty. But the circumstances had been unfavourable. In part it may have been the figure of Francis Bacon which interposed between Tobie Mathew and the chances of the royal favour. Now in his later years it was with the survivors from King James's Court that Tobie found himself most at ease; among men, his intimate friendship was reserved for Lord Treasurer Portland and Cottington, and the former's *protégé* Sir Henry Vane. The three elder men were exact contemporaries, and Portland, then Richard Weston, had entered the House of Commons in 1601 with Tobie Mathew; they had begun their careers together in the same Parliament. There is no doubt that the pleasantest period of Sir Tobie's Indian summer was that passed at Roehampton House when the Earl of Portland was lord treasurer.

Portland was an elderly cautious statesman in a

difficult position who had come in middle life to love magnificence. A heavy choleric man, he seems to have possessed a jovial facility for a relationship of equals. He had nothing of Buckingham's inexperienced patronage, nor was he moved to cheerful amusement at "littell prittie Tobie Mathew". He seems to have been lonely in the midst of a family which he was always tempted to advance. He was grateful to the King for the great marriages which he arranged for them, but there was no warmth of friendship with Charles I. He was chief minister in those years when his master was numbed after the murder of the Duke of Buckingham. His position reposed upon his usefulness and he was linked to his sovereign by that interest which he could create through his expedients. He was essentially a finance minister.

Portland was by nature cordial to solid men and had introduced Wentworth to the royal service. Superficially he was on good terms with Dr. Laud. The Queen had a tinge of hostility towards him, and her courtiers were his enemies. In his leisure he would plan his new great house and its adornment. On all these sides Sir Tobie was at hand to help him. He would catalogue the list of Portland's enemies and their discomfiture. He would conjure away each trouble. The lord treasurer's enemies, he explained on one occasion, had in their witless envy erected certain steps whereby the Earl had risen so high as to be able to see the clouds far below him. These sentences have the structure of the direction for a masque and are peculiar to Tobie Mathew. He was thus accustomed to predict the movements of court favour. Sir Thomas Roe and the Elizabethans preferred to use the analogy of the stars.

And then Tobie would join in the projects for the creation of Roehampton House. His mind turned to the embellishment of the façade, to the formal garden with its vases and to the great equestrian statue which Hubert Le Sueur was casting. Each perspective was to lead up to this gilded figure, *Carolus Magnus*. There were the paintings to be considered for the chapel which Dr. Laud was about to consecrate. The lord treasurer had a care for proprieties in Church and State. It is at this point that the question of Portland's religious outlook must be considered, for it has a bearing on the view adopted as to Tobie Mathew's character. Briefly the facts are these.

Lady Portland came of a Catholic family and her husband incurred some odium in opposition circles on that account. On his death-bed the lord treasurer was reconciled to the Church of Rome. He was alleged to have been secretly a Catholic while outwardly an Anglican, and to have been encouraged in this course of action by Tobie Mathew. This does not square with my own impression.

It seems more reasonable to suppose that Portland was aroused in his last illness from that Erastian indifference which was a commonplace of his age and class. On this reading he was throughout life a conservative royal servant paying a seemly and convenient reverence to authority. He would give the Bishop of London due respect and ask him to bless the family ceremonies. This he owed as much to his own position as to the prelate's. In matters of foreign policy he joined with those who scrutinized the King of Sweden's projects. He wished for peace and viewed the heroes cynically. Sir Tobie had expressed himself on the irruptions of Gustavus Adolphus into Germany. He stated that he looked upon a sovereign who had neither male issue nor a multitude of subjects and put reliance on auxiliaries "just as he would apprehend a storm". This suggests a viewpoint that was robust and Jacobean; it hardly went with Van Dyck's slender lords. There was a touch in all this of Francis Bacon. The outer world was looked on with detachment as the lord treasurer struggled with depleted revenue. The statue of *Carolus Magnus* was now in place. A letter has survived from Sir Tobie Mathew to Sir Henry Vane. "My Lord of Portland is in a better and clearer air of greatness than ever you saw him in." This was surely the ghost of James's Court with its well-worn hyperbole. On 13 March 1635 the lord treasurer died at Roehampton House; it was an unfortunate day for Tobie Mathew.

The change in Tobie's life is indicated by the fact that henceforth no other man would ever rise through him. Sir Henry Vane the elder is not regarded as a sensitive character and Clarendon has blackened his reputation, but as long as Tobie was at Portland's ear it was prudent to maintain polite exchanges. "The Lord Treasurer only is able to open and shut." Tobie seems to have been genuinely attached to Henry Vane. Sir John Harrington refers to his "sweetness of behaviour". Perhaps Tobie Mathew gave more sympathy than he received.

Certainly when Portland died the friendship with Henry Vane and the less intimate relation with Francis Cottington seem to have languished.

Sir Tobie still made certain casts. It is not easy to place his brief stay in Ireland as Lord Wentworth's secretary. There could in any case be practically nothing in common between the two men. Lord Carlisle died next year, the "Character of the Countess" was already circulating. In the autumn of 1636 Tobie was visiting at Hatfield. Now the sharp comment of the French ambassador began to touch him. "Sir Tobie Mathew", wrote M. de Fontenay, "a man of parts, an excellent linguist; he penetrates cabinets, he insinuates himself into all kinds of affairs." It was perhaps only in his last years at Court that this was in a measure true.

Throughout this period in Tobie's life his friendship with Lady Carlisle was a permanent although eventually a diminishing factor. It is in a way curious that Lucy, Countess of Carlisle, should have been captured by a taste for the exotic. A daughter of Northumberland, a niece of Essex, she had experienced each phase of the old court. She was shrewd and light-hearted and perhaps frustrated. Her marriage with one of King James's favourites had in time taken on the character of an alliance. It seems that the political field, its moves and secret springs, made more and more appeal to her. In the correspondence of this time the name Sempronia is given to her from "the great stateswoman" of Ben Jonson's *Catiline*. It was thus Tobie Mathew's knowledge of European procedure that proved attractive; this and his wit.

A COLLECTION OF

LETTERS,

MADE BY

Sr Tobie Mathews

Kr.

with a Character of the moſt Excellent Lady,
LUCY, *Counteſſe of*

CARLEILE:

By the ſame Author.

To which are Added many Letters of
his own, to ſeverall Perſons
OF HONOUR,

who were Contemporary with him.

LONDON,
Printed for *Henry Herringman*, and are to be
ſold at his Shop, at the ſign of the *Anchor*
in the Lower walk in the New
Exchange. 1660.

The letters which Tobie had collected as specimens of style rather than for their historical or biographical interest were edited after his death, together with the 'Character of the Countess', by John Donne the younger, son of the poet, who dedicated the book to Lady Carlisle.

In Lady Carlisle's life a sense of play and timing were both framed against a background of political manœuvre, the whole conducted with a French air. Marie de Chevreuse was here her mentor. For Lady Carlisle there seems to have been a pleasure in the fact of effort; the gaining of the Queen's friendship; the gaining of Lord Strafford's confidence; the final subjugation of Mr. Pym. It may have been a key to her character that she loved the arduous. The portraits show her slender, with a brittle grace; she was deft and challenging; easily bored, I think, by poets like Carew and D'Avenant. Within these limits she was very loyal; undoubtedly she meant much to Tobie Mathew.

The ending of the friendship appears to have been gradual. She severed many ties when she went out from the court to make Pym's cause her own. She left behind her the appurtenances gathered through the years, the young poets and the ageing wits. Among the latter, and once so close to her, was Tobie Mathew.

His enemies were now gathering. Archbishop Laud had always disapproved of him and appears to have blamed him for the lord treasurer's defection. The results of his failure to conciliate the Queen were by this time apparent; as one consequence the younger men who formed her circle did not spare their ageing senior. Thus Sir John Suckling has a reference in his *Session of the Poets* to Tobie Mathew "whispering nothing in somebody's ear". He was also associated in the public mind with Endymion Porter's wife and her busy convert-making.

Fourteen years ago I took the view that Tobie Mathew was both intimate and at ease with the group of ladies belonging to Buckingham's family who had become Catholics. Now, after further reading, I doubt if this was so. Endymion Porter and Tobie had certain points in common, a knowledge of Spanish and an understanding of the structure of life in Spain and Italy. But the letters that passed between the two and now survive belong mainly to the period of the Spanish Marriage project, and it does not seem probable that the association lasted with any strength into the later period. Certainly it is clear that Tobie Mathew can have had very little in common with the three papal agents Panzani, Con and Rossetti, who came in succession to reside at Charles's Court. There was perhaps a certain link with Rossetti, who was a young ecclesiastic of varied accomplishments, but there is some evidence to show that he viewed Con with positive dislike. In all three cases the judgments of these agents were superficial and coloured by a tiresome optimism, while Tobie had a range of knowledge and experience of English matters with which they were unable to compete. And then it is so clear that the Queen never cared for him.

During these years Tobie Mathew's name was coupled with that of Walter Montague, a young diplomat more than twenty years his junior. In fact they belonged to different circles. Montague, a younger son of the first Earl of Manchester, then lord privy seal, was wholly French in all his sympathies, had been received into the Catholic Church in France and was an intimate dependant of Queen

Henrietta's. These points are necessary to explain the difficulty into which Sir Tobie fell in the autumn of 1637. One of Buckingham's nieces, Lady Newport, became a Catholic and her husband appealed to the Archbishop alleging that Walter Montague and Tobie Mathew had been the instruments of this change. Their banishment from the realm was demanded. It is generally agreed that the movers in this conversion were, to describe them as George Gerrard the letter-writer sets them down, "my Lady Duchess of Buckingham, her [Lady Newport's] sister Porter, and Seignior Con". But Laud accepted the accusation and brought the matter to the King. An extract from a letter sent by Lord Conway to Lord Deputy Wentworth gives a glimpse of the malice by which Tobie was surrounded during his last years in England. "When", he explains, "my Lord of Newport's matter was debated at the Council Table the King did use such words of Wat Montague and Sir Tobie Mathew that the fright made Wat keep his chamber longer than his sickness would have detained him, and Don Tobiah was in such perplexity that I find he will make a very ill man to be a martyr." The words that follow indicate dislike. "But now the dog doth again wag his tail."

The tension, which would endure until the outbreak of the Civil Wars some five years later, was already growing, and it was not only the Puritan opposition which was anxious to disembarrass itself of the Catholics associated with the Court. The Anglican Royalists early felt that these men could be offered up as an acceptable sacrifice. And then by this time Tobie Mathew was certainly a priest and as such outside the law. An entry in the Beaufort MSS. at Badminton should be mentioned here for it creates a rather confusing impression. In a detailed account of the household at Raglan Castle this note appears: "Sir Toby Mathew the first chaplain." This is a solitary reference and apparently dates from the Civil Wars. Sir Tobie's name does not appear in the correspondence of either the first or the second Marquess of Worcester. The latter was the author of the *Century of Inventions* and proposed, among other more fanciful projects, a steam pumping engine. It would have been interesting had Tobie Mathew provided a link between Francis Bacon's experiments and those which Worcester and Caspar Kaltoff carried out. Possibly he never took up the post at Raglan; the note may have been a draft for an establishment which did not materialize.

In these last years before the conflict Tobie Mathew was over sixty and far away from real politics. His association with his friends in the convents of the Low Countries grew closer. He was getting elderly, as were the members of his circle Elizabeth Lady Falkland and Elizabeth Lady Thurles, who was married to his cousin George Mathew of Radyr; he had now re-discovered his Welsh relations. He employed himself in writing the account of his conversion which has been so often quoted in this short sketch. He had begun it at the instance of Dame Mary Gage, a member of the English Benedictine community at Brussels. As the storm gathered, the manuscript took on increasingly the character of a justification. As such it was bequeathed to his cousin's family. It passed first to Lady Thurles's elder son by her second marriage, Theobald Mathew (known as Toby), and then to the latter's grandson George Mathew, who was married to Mary Lady Shelley, a grand-niece of Dame Mary Gage. Their son, another George Mathew, gave it to Alban Butler the hagiographer.

The work had gone forward slowly, for it was only finished on 8 September 1640. On that day Sir Tobie wrote in his London lodgings the last page of his manuscript, in which he counted up his blessings.

"And upon the whole matter", he wrote, "I can, without vanity, and may, with much gratitude to God, affirm that I have never been either in want or near it; but my hands have always been full of money, and my fortune far superior to my expense; and so my mind at ease. And, in fine, I have been ever the more able to lend my friends my service in that kind than obliged to expect it from them.

"My country I lost many years, which yet God gave me life and health to expect; and he also raised me friends, whereby I recovered it; and amongst whom I enjoy it with as much honour and advantage of many kinds, as any man of my poor condition hath received. . . . So that these things may well be able to teach that part of the world, which shall hereafter come to understand of my little story, how they are to cast themselves headlong into the hands of God."

To this he added those pages which he entitled *Posthumus* and signed on the same day. "I find myself", he began, "so daily subject to indispositions and infirmities, and so full also of years, which now pass three-score, as to give me good assurance that my life is not to last very long. So that it imports me enough to consider well what things I may esteem it fit to deliver myself of, before I die." Coming to the burden of the accusations against him he made his own position clear. "I take God to witness that I have never, in my whole life, known any one subject of the King's, in this kingdom, receive any one pension, or any other pecuniary profit, of any Prince in Europe; for I mean not to make it my business now to consider whether any of our seminaries or monasteries have any pensions from Popes or Princes, or no, towards the breeding of priests for the mission of England."

And then he comes to the accusations against his loyalty. "And as for our not being *good* subjects, and carrying disaffections, or having ill designs against the King or State; I take God most solemnly to witness that I never, or so much as probably heard, of any disloyal purpose, which was harboured by any subject of the King's, either at home or abroad, against his person or crown, his prosperity or his safety, in any kind at all, or in the least degree; except only such few as were publicly known, and were convicted, and suffered for it in the sight of the world."

On 16 November 1640 the two Houses joined in petitioning for Sir Tobie Mathew's banishment.

The last years of his life were passed in retirement in the Low Countries; he died on 13 October 1655 in the English College at Ghent.

And now I can attempt a guess at Tobie's character. He had through all his middle age an individual piety. His real interest had always lain in the world about him, and this he conveyed by his sympathy and swift perceptions. He understood the Latin world too well to be acceptable to his countrymen, who had no desire to explore that alien territory. He attracted and was in turn attracted by all those who had a wit which was expressed in the cultivated idiom. He was in that sense responsive to his own European epoch; he *dated* quickly. Before he left England for the last time his expressions and some of his ideas were quite outmoded. He had tenacious loyalties and deep attachments; in his friendships he was devoted and generous. He was, in spite of all his activity, a spectator. The enduring influence was Francis Bacon; his life was coloured by this association more than he knew. He was always searching for those who would have been acceptable companions in those conversations on the marble seats between the hornbeams at Gorhambury.